PUERTO RICO

Text by
A. Carleen Hawn

Photos by
Andrea Pistolesi

B BONECHI

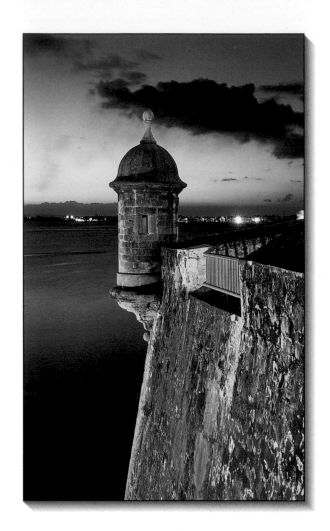

INTRODUCTION

The beautiful island of **Puerto Rico** was first discovered by Christopher Columbus in 1493 on his second sojourn into the New World. After landing at Aguadilla on the western shore, Columbus named the island **San Juan Bautista**, after St. John The Baptist. The island was renamed Puerto Rico, meaning **rich port**, in 1521. Located southeast of the larger islands of the **Greater Antilles**: present day Cuba; Jamaica; and Hispaniola, home to Haiti and the Dominican Republic, Puerto Rico sits at the virtual center of the Caribbean archipelago. Both for the sake of its key position and natural resources, the island quickly became a contested asset of Europe's colonial powers, namely the Dutch and British. Of the first settlements to be established on the island were **Caparra**, **Fajardo**, and **Boquerón**, all of which took on the traffic of military navies as well as marauding pirates. But for minor occupations by the British in the 16th Century, Spanish sovereignty of the island was sustained until the late 19th Century. Puerto Rico was granted ''a measure of autonomy'' by the crown in 1897 and then finally ceded to the United States after the **Spanish-American War of 1898**, but this did not end its ''colonial'' status which has continued to evolve.

In **1900** Puerto Rico was officially recognized by the U.S. Congress as an **unincorporated territory** of the **United States**. In **1917** residents here were granted full **U.S. citizenship**. Not all of them claimed it. The island's current status as a **Commonwealth,** which permits it to have its own constitution and a representative government, was officiated first in 1952. There has been much debate, both in Puerto Rico and in the U.S. Congress, over making the island the 51st state, but in 1993 the Puerto Rican people voted to retain their commonwealth status. As such, they pay no U.S. taxes, but do benefit enormously from Big Brother's economic assistance. Geographically diverse, the island is bisected by the mountain range known as the **Cordillera Central**, forged out of seismic eruptions deep beneath the ocean floor millions of years ago. This same geology accounts for the lovely, though often treacherous, **coral reefs** and **cays** that pepper the waters off Puerto Rico's coast. While the southwestern side of the island remains relatively dry due to the Cordillera's rain shadow, the eastern flank enjoys so much moisture as to boast one of the Caribbean's only **real tropical rain forests**. Wildlife preservation is prevalent here, evidence of a community proud of and intent on protecting the island's uniquely diverse resources and habitat.

Industry on the island was traditionally and has remained largely agricultural. **Sugarcane** and **pineapple plantations** are literally omnipresent. **Rum distilleries**, which include the famed brand name **Bacardi**, benefited from the sugar boom at the turn of the century and have brought the island's name recognition ever since. The **fishing industry** is another mainstay of the island's economy, particularly on the western shore where canneries operated by **StarKist**, **Bumble Bee**, and **Caribe Tuna** are located. Together, they are responsible for nearly all of the tuna imported into the U.S. annually.

Commercial development, particularly in the banking district of San Juan's **Hato Rey**, has turned the island into a **banking center** for the Antilles. Interior developments, like the construction of the first trans-island highway connecting Ponce to San Juan, when taken in tandem with the numerous **state sponsored preservation projects** of Puerto Rico's historic cities, have deftly helped to bring the island up to speed with the outside world while at the same time made great strides in securing the continuation of its rich historical heritage. By these accounts, coupled with an aggressively cultivated tourist industry, the tiny island of Puerto Rico has been brought out onto the international fore: in **1979** the **Pan American Games** were held in San Juan and in **1986** Pope John Paul II paid a highly publicized and cherished visit.

San Juan itself has grown to a population of **1.6 million**. In addition to its **tropical amenities** and **resort townships**, this bustling city is often credited as an incubator of intellectual and artistic fervor. San Juan plays host to **several universities**, has a countless number of **art galleries** and **museums**, and its streets are, quite literally, filled with the celebratory **music** of the Caribbean, day and night. Some of the world's greatest writers, performers, and artists including, Salvador Brau, José Campeche, José De Diego, René Marquéz, Francisco Oller, Alejandro Tapia y Rivera and Manuel Zeno Gandía, were Puerto Rican natives. Still others immigrated here to benefit from San Juan's culturally rich mecca. Other Puerto Ricans of international acclaim include performers Chita Rivera, Jimmy Smits, Rita Moreno and the late Raul Julia.

OLD SAN JUAN

*F*ounded in 1521, at the height of the 16th Century Spanish Empire, **San Juan** is one of the oldest of the colonial cities in the Western Hemisphere. It has served as Puerto Rico's commercial and military capital for over four centuries. The European influence is most visible in the **historic district** of **Old San Juan**, located on the city's northwestern peninsula. Just several blocks in size, Old San Juan is bordered on either side by two **military forts**: *El Morro* on the westernmost tip and **San Cristóbal** on the eastern side. Serving as both "the first and last safe harbor" in the West Indies, the forts were commissioned by the crown in order to protect the traffic of Armada vessels which moored in the **Bay of San Juan**, many of them laden with treasures reaped from the New World.

Literally hundreds of the buildings are historic landmarks, producing a melange of **Spanish colonial architecture**. With its iron-paved lamplit streets and pastel plastered dwellings, the district evokes all the aesthetic charm of European cities like Paris, Madrid, or Prague. In 1973 Old San Juan was declared a **World Heritage Site** by the **UNESCO**, an honor similarly bestowed on landmarks including the Pyramids of Giza, the Taj Mahal, and Versailles. It is here, in Old San Juan, nestled amongst the narrow streets and passageways, that the bulwark of San Juan's famed **art galleries** is located, along with a significant number of its **churches**, **parks**, and most popular **nightspots**. Heavily touristed as it is, the best way to experience the quaintess of Old San Juan is to wander about on foot which, despite its size, will likely take more than a day.

Right: A view of El Morro's lower ramparts, including the string of cannon emplacements that line the lower walls overlooking the entryway to the port.

Preceding pages: This striking panoramic offers a bird's-eye-view of El Morro in its entirety. Not only does this best represent the fortress' immense size and defensive architecture, but also its strategic importance perched high above Old San Juan and the city's bustling port.

Bottom: Again, a full aerial view of the fortress' main structure. Positioned as it is, on the very tip of San Juan's northwesternmost peninsula, the fort serves as both guardian to the city and gateway to the Atlantic Ocean.

CASTILLO SAN FELIPE DEL MORRO

This military fortress, the **Castillo San Felipe Del Morro** commonly referred to simply as **El Morro**, is perched dramatically atop a rocky promontory at the northwesternmost tip of the old city's peninsula and stands guard over the interior gateway to **Bahía de San Juan**, the **Bay of San Juan**. The massive triangular stone structure includes six different levels of **ramparts** and **gun batteries** and took nearly two hundred years to build. Financed by the Spain, it is one of the largest fortress in the Caribbean area. Begun in 1540 as a single battery installment, El Morro was not completed in its present form until 1787. This first battery, a solitary round tower, still stands on the upper level of El Morro's interior.

The **exterior walls** surrounding El Morro are nearly twenty feet thick and reach heights exceeding 140 feet above the Atlantic waters beneath the garrison's clifftop base. From the fort itself these walls connect to similar fortifications along the southern and northern shores and span to encircle the entirety of Old San Juan. For these defenses Old San Juan came to be known as *"La Ciudad Murada"*, **the walled city**.

El Morro was attacked repeatedly by the other colonial powers, including Britain, Holland and France, as well as various marauding pirate ships in the unebbing contest for control over the New World. But for brief intervals, El Morro was not fully relinquished until the American navy overran San Juan during the **Spanish-American War of 1898**. Not surprisingly, El Morro, like Old San Juan, is honored as a **UNESCO World Heritage Site**.

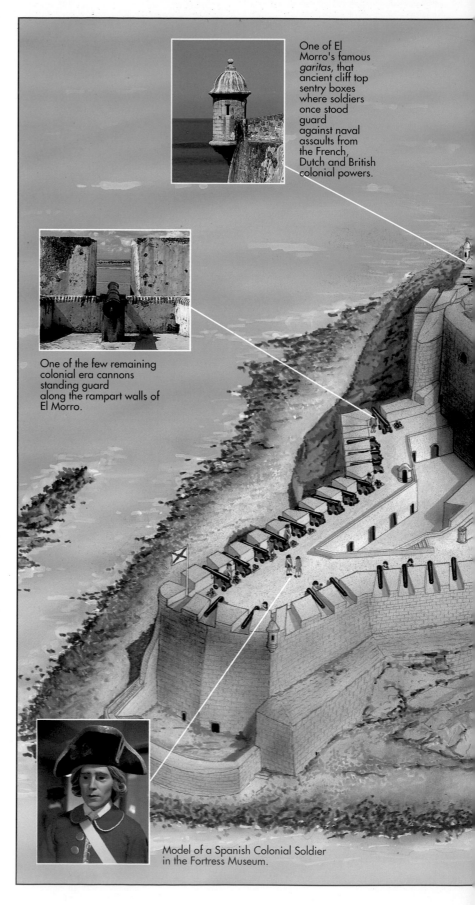

One of El Morro's famous *garitas*, that ancient cliff top sentry boxes where soldiers once stood guard against naval assaults from the French, Dutch and British colonial powers.

One of the few remaining colonial era cannons standing guard along the rampart walls of El Morro.

Model of a Spanish Colonial Soldier in the Fortress Museum.

The charming Port of San Juan Lighthouse, located on El Morro's upper ramparts.

This red-domed chapel forms the centerpiece of the San Juan Cemetery located downhill from El Morro on the northern shore of Old San Juan.

One of El Morro's dramatic, corniced doorways along the main plaza of the upper ramparts.

The dramatic courtyard and arched gateway that make up El Morro's main plaza.

9

CAMPO EL MORRO

Ascending to El Morro from the township, one must cross the former **drill square**, a grassy expanse nearly **30 acres in size**, known as **Campo El Morro**. For its strategic slope, Campo El Morro was likely intended as a defensive barrier between the fort and its residential patrons. In any case, it presents a dramatic entry to these impressive bastions. Today the **field** is used more often by picnickers and kite enthusiasts both for the sake of its panoramic ocean and bay views, as well as the high winds rising off the coastal bluff.

A view of Campo El Morro from the southern township side of the grassy slope, near the military barracks. Formerly used as a drill yard by troops stationed here, the massive length and width of the lawn (best demonstrated in this shot) also made it a significant strategic defense against military assaults from the town.

The monument in this photo stands mid-field, along the footpath leading to the formal entry of the fort. It is one of the many such monuments documenting the historic significance of the fort and pays homage to the soldiers that served and died here between the 16th and 18th centuries.

Inside the fortress, just outside the yellow arched walls of the main courtyard which it predates, is this second plaza complete with El Morro's original single-tower battery, around which the rest of the complex was built.

A close-up of the doorway exposes the architectural refinements present throughout the fortress, particularly on its many portals, including this crest and sconce honoring the Spanish Monarchy.

Three views of the fortress' courtyard and main plaza: The vaulted gateway and superficial arches along the plaza walls initiate an aesthetic pattern repeated throughout the fort, most notable along the tops of its exterior ramparts. The brilliant yellow and white stucco finish is, however, unique to this portion of the fort adding drama and flare to this, El Morro's most formal arena.

MAIN PLAZA

From the green, the pathway leading into El Morro's **inner courtyard** spans an interior **dry moat** followed by a dramatic vaulted archway of yellow and white stucco which forms the formal gateway to the fortress' garrison and **main plaza**. Above this archway fly three flags, the Puerto Rican national flag, the American flag and the flag of San Juan.

From here, the central courtyard, begins the labyrinthine system of artillery ramps and passageways which lead intermittently to various dungeons and vaults underground, the soldiers' quarters, and strategic guard outposts throughout the fortress.

Following the central ramp of the main courtyard down to the area of the lower ramparts, one arrives at the **Santa Barbara Bastion**. Santa Barbara offers one of the most dramatic of El Morro's panoramas with its oceanside precipice.

Right: A view of El Morro's charming lighthouse, also known as Port of San Juan Lighthouse, just outside the main plaza.

LIGHTHOUSE

Back on the upper rampart, follow a second artillery ramp down from the main courtyard, this one towards the **Port of San Juan Lighthouse** on the northern side of the fort. The Lighthouse, which has protected the gateway to the harbor for over two hundred years, was destroyed once by an American mortar shell during the Spanish-American War of 1898. It has since been restored. It stands at the highest point of any of El Morro's many ramparts and, with its blackened brick walls and white trim, the lighthouse is easily visible from all sides.

Capilla El Morro, the modest sanctuary where soldiers frequently prayed before going into battle.

Left: A view of one of El Morro's many vaulted passageways deep within the fortress' walls. This one displays colonial armament: a cannon which likely stood amongst the wedge-shaped emplacements that line the rampart walls.

CAPILLA EL MORRO

Deep inside the fort's inner walls is the charming yet austere **chapel** once used by the officers and soldiers stationed here. Without a conventional altar, there is no visible crucifix or other religious relic, merely a painting of the Madonna shown here standing guard over her faithful Christian crusaders. Simple as this one is, the presence of chapels like these is evidence of the religious piety of the Spaniards who took the pre-eminence of their faith in the New World. The Spaniards and their missionaries proselytized to the Indians, killed in Puerto Rico very soon after the colonization. This accounts in large part for the predominance of Catholicism throughout the Antilles and Latin America today.

MUSEUM

Located just inside the main gateway of the central courtyard, on the upper rampart of the fortress' are a **museum** and a **souvenir shop**. The museum, complete with model installations of historic Armada vessels and replicas of colonial and military dress, offers a comprehensive history of El Morro and the evolution of this massive military installation. An **informational video** as well as **guided tours** are offered daily here, in English and Spanish. Both are free of charge.

Three installations of the El Morro museum: A colonial soldier in full uniform; a Sanjuanero in folk garb; and a full replica of one of the many ships of the Spanish Armada.

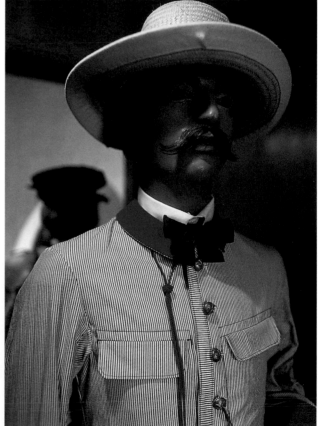

Top left: The protectorate as the soldiers saw it. A panoramic view of the lower rampart and exterior cannon emplacements as seen from the interior of El Morro. So great were the fortress' defenses that, it was said, no ship within view, no matter how far out to sea, was out of range for the guns.

Lower left: A continuation of the rail on which the cannon was moved adds an element of artistry to this already impressive structure.

Above: A close-up of the cannon emplacements overlooking the Atlantic surf beneath El Morro's northern wall.

CANNON EMPLACEMENTS

The **wedge shaped hollows** which pepper the top of El Morro's massive walls were the strategic **installation points** for the massive **cannons** used to defend the fortress against invading navies. These guns, stationed literally back-to-back along the v-shaped waterfront arm of the fort's lower rampart perimeter, created an almost unbreachable line of defense. So powerful were these guns, they were said to have been able to fire on any ship within the fortress' field of vision, no matter how far out at sea. It is worth noting that the few times El Morro was overrun, it came from advances on the southern township side, like the advance staged by Britain's Lord Cumberland from El Condado in 1595, but never from the waterfront.

But strategics aside, the stonework along the rampart tops figure prominently in the architectural integrity of El Morro. The interweaving pattern of arches which trim the base of each cannon emplacement mirror the vaulted arches which line the central gateway and courtyard above, as well as the structure of the fortress' interior passageways. Even still, out along the ramparts, they are beautiful as though they were a decoration.

Top left: This dramatic arched portal graces the peak of one of El Morro's many steep artillery ramps leading down to still another of the fortress' mighty ramparts. This one is located on the south western side of the fortress facing the bay.

Bottom left: A close-up of the cannon emplacements, here, overlooking the inlet waters leading into Bahía de San Juan.

Above: A dramatic approach to one of El Morro's charming garitas, the solitary sentry boxes that punctuate the fort walls hanging out high above the cliffs.

The multitude of **artillery ramps** and vaulted passageways that connect El Morro's different levels provide an attractive framework for photographs, even as one is at risk of getting lost among them. The sheer incline of these corridors is as impressive as their architectural layout. One can imagine how difficult it must have been to transport the heavy guns and artillery up and down these pathways, particularly in the heat of battle.
The charming rounded **sentry boxes** that are perched at the end points of El Morro's walls are referred to as *garitas*. Their domed caps give the *garitas*, one could say, the resemblance of a helmeted soldier. They can be found at other forts in San Juan, like the **Castillo de San Cristóbal** on the other side of Old San Juan. Again, they are an artifice of the architectural and strategic creativity displayed here. Jetting out over the water as they do at El Morro, the *garitas* have come to be one of the most photographed symbols of Puerto Rico.

SAN JUAN CEMETERY

Again, on the northern shore of El Morro's peninsula, further downside from the Lighthouse, lies the historic necropolis known as **San Juan Cemetery**. Settled on a grassy promontory between El Morro's huge walls and the rocky cliffs above the Atlantic surf, the cemetery is, as its reputation claims, perhaps one of the most picturesque of burial grounds anywhere.
With its quintessential earthtop tombs, nearly all of them bleached to a brightening white glare, and adorned with standing crosses or other Christian symbols, it truly is a beautiful, if somewhat ominous, place. The interior wall, which stands against the base of El Morro's fortification, is a vaulted arcade which forms an additional decorative backdrop to this already awesome setting. But the **centerpiece** of the cemetery is a lovely circular, red-domed **chapel** which dates back to the late 19th Century.
From the eastern edge of the cemetery, looking westward towards El Morro, the chapel's silhouette is slightly eclipsed by the rounded top of the Port of San Juan Lighthouse on the horizon and the Atlantic to the north.

Above: Ballajá Barracks, the large yellow and white stuccoed building pictured above served as the soldiers' quarters during the colonial era. Today it houses the Museo de las Américas, and its large open-air plaza serves as a resting place for tourists preparing for the long ascent up Campo El Morro.

Right: Two views of the historic Casa Blanca, the first governor's house of Old San Juan, located at the corner of Calle del Morro and Calle San Sebastián.

BALLAJÁ

Down from El Morro proper, back across the expanse of the training field to the southeast, stands an enormous yellow and white building, in the same tradition as the fortress' decorative courtyard, which served as the soldiers' quarters during the colonial era.

Transformed into a hospital after the U.S. took Puerto Rico, the **Cuartel de Ballajá**, or **Ballajá Barracks**, cuts a stunning image at the foot of its gothic parent, El Morro. As the centerpiece of a hundred million dollar restoration project for the district of Old San Juan, the historic barracks will figure even more prominently in the future.

Today, the Ballajá Barracks house the **Museo de las Américas**, **Museum of the Américas**. One of Old San Juan's finest museums, it represents the multi-cultural history and development of the West Indies throughout the colonial era.

CASA BLANCA

Yet another of Old San Juan's historic landmarks, this one known as **Casa Blanca**, sits at the foot of the El Morro training field. Originally built in 1521, Casa Blanca, as its name would imply, is a simple white washed stucco dwelling. It was erected for use as residence by the Spanish explorer, **Juan Ponce de León**, though he never actually lived here. Ponce de León served as Puerto Rico's first governor beginning in 1508. Prior to the installation of El Morro, which it predates by nearly two decades, Casa Blanca was also meant to be used as a stronghold by the early settlers against the attacks of hostile Indians. La Fortaleza, built eleven years later, in 1532, soon replaced Casa Blanca as the governor's residence. Casa Blanca remained the residence of Ponce de León's family until the late 18th Century. Today it houses a **museum** and the **Institute for Advanced Studies**.

A beautiful San Juan sunset eclipses the famed sculpture installation known as La Rogativa. Located along Recinto del Oeste, the sculpture commemorates a failed siege levied against the city in 1797.

PLAZA DE LA ROGATIVA

Walking along the westernmost promenade of Old San Juan, **Recinto del Oeste**, visitors will come across the sculpture installation known as **La Rogativa**. But more than just an impressive piece of modern art, **La Rogativa** is an outstanding example of this city's cultural underpinnings, both religious and historic. The sculpture was commissioned to commemorate a failed siege against the city levied by the British under Sir Ralph Ambercrombie in 1797. Legend has it that after failing initially to take San Juan, Sir Ambercrombie enforced a naval blockade, cutting off San Juan and its residents from Spanish reinforcements. The Spanish governor, after seeing his troops and subjects suffer for weeks, is said to have called for a *rogativa* or **divine**

intervention from the Christian Saints. The women of San Juan, in a dramatic display of faith, then banned together and marched through the city bearing torches and sounding makeshift instruments. Whether a dogmatic ritual or an amateurish conceit, Sir Ambercrombie is said to have mistaken the procession for the arrival of reinforcement troops. He apparently fled the island for fear that he was outmanned.

The **sculpture**, erected on the plaza where the religious marched transpired, shows two women, torches in hand, side by side with a staff-bearing bishop. It stands as a tribute both to the women, the legend, and the historic religious fortitude of the Puerto Rican people.

LA FORTALEZA

Further down **Calle Recinto del Oeste**, where the avenue meets **Calle Fortaleza**, is the historic gubernatorial residence from which Calle Fortaleza gets its name: **La Fortaleza, "the fortress"**. Begun in 1532, La Fortaleza was erected to replace Casa Blanca as the home of Puerto Rico's governor. It was completed eight years later, in 1540.
A much larger and more splendorous residence, La Fortaleza is still used today as the governor's mansion, making it the oldest inhabited executive mansion in the Western Hemisphere.
Built on an oceanfront promontory, the architects of La Fortaleza quickly perceived a strategic flaw: unlike Casa Blanca before it, the house, due to its ill-conceived location, would be indefensible. Not coincidentally, the construction of El Morro high up on the rocky bluff overlooking San Juan, was commenced later that same year. Thus protected, La Fortaleza has stood the test of time. The architectural beauty of **La Fortaleza** has

An aerial view of La Fortaleza, historic and present-day residence of the governor of Puerto Rico, also exposes the waterfront promenade and the red stuccoed Gate of San Juan, the original entryway into the Old City. Beyond, the rest of Old San Juan and cruise ships at port in the Bahía de San Juan.

Left: Again, an aerial view of La Fortaleza. Here the internal and external fortifications of this pale blue, fairytale fortress, including the 16th Century watch towers and the original walls of "La Ciudad Murada" are best demonstrated-along with some decidedly more modern amenities on the roof.

Top: Viewed in profile, the stuccoed façade of La Fortaleza literally blends into the late afternoon sky. Here, Puerto Rico's ubiquitous garitas appear again along the wall and promenade to better secure the fortress.

also sustained itself. The large pristinely white and pale blue stucco "fortress" stands above the massive stone wall of the city like a medieval castle. In fact, a pair of the original 16th Century **watch towers** remain on the waterside corners of the structure. The rest of the mansion, updated over the last several centuries incorporates many different architectural styles including a 19th Century façade complete with **beveled glass windows** and **neo-classical decorative columns** in the courtyard. The interior is particularly ornate, a mixture of Baroque, Gothic, and even Arabian aesthetic inspiration. Just as El Morro and the Old City of San Juan, La Fortaleza is recognized by the UNESCO as a

World Heritage Site. The wood finishings of the mansion as well as portions of its interior structure make use of a native-grown wood called *ausubo*, or **ironwood**. The windows of La Fortaleza, like many other buildings in Old San Juan are trimmed in European inspired **iron works**. In the case of La Fortaleza's courtyard, **rich wood shutters** are employed, evoking a kind of Renaissance appeal. Eclectic as it is, the walls surrounding La Fortaleza complete this architectural medley with the charming *garitas* or **sentry boxes**, seen most prominently at El Morro, repeat themselves here along the waterfront outer-walls behind the mansion.

Above: An aerial view of Old San Juan's most romantic promenade, Paseo de la Princesa. Here the Paseo is seen from the bay front rotunda as it stretches along Calle San Justo beneath the Old City walls and all the way to Plaza de la Marina.

Top right: The stunning fountain at the center of the Paseo's rotunda pays homage to the diverse ethnic origins of Puerto Rico: Spanish, Indian, and African.

Bottom right: Another view of the Paseo as it stretches along the tree-lined Calle San Justo. The grey and white stuccoed building along the street houses a former prison garrison (also called La Princesa), numerous gift shops, a tourist office and a museum. Here too are several of the outdoor eateries and coffee shops for which the Paseo is famous.

PASEO DE LA PRINCESA

South from La Fortaleza, forming the southern border of Old San Juan is probably the most romantic promenade in the historic district: **Paseo de la Princesa**. It begins with a dramatic rotunda that surrounds a large circular fountain and esplanade on the western waterfront. The **fountain**, yet another example of San Juan's artistic patronage, is a modern installation of three humans: a Spaniard, an Indian and an African, meant to depict the ethnic origins of Puerto Rico. The human figures are surrounded by dolphins, meant to conjure up images of the island's organic union with the surrounding ocean. It is one of **several sculpture installations** along the promenade

including another representing a beloved former mayor of San Juan, **Felisa Rincón de Gautier**, who governed here from 1946-1968.

From the waterfront's fountain, the Paseo skirts the old city walls and extends east, from **Calle San Justo**, for nearly three blocks until it reaches the **Plaza de la Marina**. Along this eastward stretch the Paseo passes a former prison garrison also known as **La Princesa**. Today La Princesa is building, houses, the **Puerto Rican Department of Tourism** and a **museum**. This stretch also provides several outdoor amenities including **restaurants** and **mini parks**. Paseo de la Princesa is particularly famous for its **gazebo eateries** including **créole outposts** and

A twilight view of the waterfront promenade which surrounds Old San Juan beneath its massive walls.

Left: One of the many European-inspired iron work street lamps which line Old San Juan's streets and promenades giving it the rich, romantic flavor for which it is known.

PROMENADE ALONG THE OLD CITY

The **waterfront promenades** that extend **beneath the exterior walls** of the old city, particularly the **Paseo de la Princesa**, with their lamplit atmosphere offer the best of romantic strolling paths from which to admire both the ocean sunsets and the dramatic profile of Old San Juan. Stretching northward from the fountain, along the western wall of the old city, the Paseo de la Princesa procures the perfect route for a wayward walking tour of the old city leading visitors past such notable landmarks as the **Casa Blanca**, **La Fortaleza**, and the **Puerta de San Juan**. Past this point, the Paseo finally merges with the **Calle del Recinto Oeste**.

The luminous rococo interior of Capilla del Cristo, Chapel of Christ, is made so by a gold and silver altarpiece and the decorative paintings by native Sanjuanero, José Campeche, who lived and worked here.

CAPILLA DEL CRISTO

Situated above the old city wall, directly behind Paseo de la Princesa, is the famed **Capilla del Cristo** or **Chapel of Christ**. As with many historic landmarks in Old San Juan, the Chapel of Christ is steeped in island legend. This one says that in 1753, during a horse race of one of the island's annual "fiestas", a young male rider lost control of his horse and plunged, seemingly to his death, into the bay below. By some token of religious faith and certainly part miracle, a bystander is said to have called on Christ for intercession. The church was built both to commemorate the tragedy and to block off the point of Calle del Cristo from which he is supposed to have met his demise.

The chapel is lovely to see and worth a visit. It has a unique set of **glass doors** which display an ornate **gold and silver altar** and the chapel's **Campeche paintings** are easily visible from the street.

CALLE DEL CRISTO

Widely held as the most quintessential byway of Old San Juan, **Calle del Cristo** or **Christ's Street**, lies just one block inland from Calle Recinto del Oeste. Calle del Cristo runs north and south, ascending towards the base of the grounds of El Morro. In its route this charming avenue leads past some of Old San Juan's finest **colonial architecture** including its most **picturesque residences** displaying a variety of **pastel stucco shades**, all with the **iron window trimmings** and **flower boxes** that this romantic district is known for.

Some of Old San Juan's most historic sites are also located on Calle del Cristo, most of them at the northern end. They include: the famed **San Juan Cathedral**, the **Plaza de San José**, and the **San Juan Dominican Convent**.

Also along **Calle del Cristo**, directly opposite the San Juan Cathedral is the beautiful luxury hotel, **Gran Hotel El Convento**. It was originally established in 1651 as a convent for the Carmelites, an order of Catholic nuns. The nuns later moved out of Old San Juan to the town of **Santurce** which today is part of the municipality of San Juan. Sometime in the mid 1950's the former convent was converted to the current hotel whose austere interior still retains the influence of its original inhabitants.

Below: The lovely Gran Hotel El Convento, located halfway down Calle del Cristo, was constructed as a Convent for the Carmelite nuns in the mid-17th Century. Today, the convent (El Convento as the cornice inscription reads) plays host to a luxury hotel.

Above: This wall of adoquines, *bricks, which backs a small square off Calle del Cristo, has slowly been taken over by nesting pigeons, thus fostering the name Parque de las Palomas, or Pigeon Park, as the square is commonly known.*

Right: Visitors and locals visit Parque de las Palomas to rest in the shade and enjoy the view of Bahía de San Juan, to picnic or, of course, to feed the tourist-friendly pigeons.

PARQUE DE LAS PALOMAS

At the southern end of Calle del Cristo set just opposite Capilla del Cristo, is one of Old San Juan's most famous parks: **Parque de las Palomas** or the **Pigeon Park** as it is colloquially named. The wall of *adoquines*, bricks, in the city wall along the back of the park is famous as a **nesting habitat** for literally thousands of pigeons from which the park now derives its name. Set against the gradual slope of Calle del Cristo, the park also offers a lovely **vista** of the bay below. It makes for a popular spot for **picnics**, or merely for an afternoon **siesta** in visitors' romantic **walking tours** of the old city.

Left: An aerial view of the magnificent San Juan Cathedral as it fronts Calle del Cristo.

Above: The cathedral is famous for its trompe-l'oeil *decor which graces the transept ceiling under the central dome and cupolas.*

CATEDRAL DE SAN JUAN

The **Catedral de San Juan** is undoubtedly one of the most important houses of worship in Puerto Rico. It fronts Calle del Cristo, half way up the hill, where the avenue meets **Caleta de San Juan**. Like many of Old San Juan's architectural wonders, the Cathedral's beautiful beige and white stucco structure displays more than one aesthetic period. It was begun in 1540, but the current facade was not added until the early 19th Century.

Resemblant of many **Renaissance** Basilicas, the facade is subdivided into three tiers, each with decorative **neo-classical columns** and central **sculpture-bearing portals**. The red and white dome and matching **cupolas** on either end of the transept roof are fixtures of the San Juan skyline. The interior of the cathedral is also impressive, though more ornate, fashioning a *trompe-l'oeil* **ceiling** done in earth tones. Many of Puerto Rico's most important religious relics are installed inside the Cathedral, including the remains of **Ponce de León**, which were entombed beneath the transept in the early 20th Century–some four hundred years after he died in 1521. There is a statue of **La Virgen de la Providencia**, Puerto Rico's patron saint, and a chapel in the Cathedral's right nave dedicated to the **Souls in Purgatory**.

Also facing the Cathedral off Calle del Cristo is the **Plaza de las Monjas**, or **Nuns Square**, a good place to rest and cool off.

Some views of Calle del Cristo. Top left and right: The rainbow of pastel facades, which line Calle del Cristo, are undoubtedly the best demonstration of Old San Juan's eclectic colonial architecture. Here their colors are highlighted at dusk.

Bottom left: A quintessential representation of the charming iron works which decorate nearly all the stucco buildings: balconies, streetlamps, flowers boxes, and all.

Bottom right: A view of the cobble stoned Calle del Cristo as it stretches downhill to the waterfront looking out and over the Paseo de la Princesa.

Walk in either direction past the Cathedral along **Calle del Cristo** and see, yet again, some of Old San Juan's most beautiful **colonial Spanish architecture**. The cobblestoned portions of the street are offset by the pastel stucco facades and **iron lanterns** that adorn the building walls. Flowering **balconies** and **ornate cornice roof tops** fashion a romantic canopy for the old city's skyline profile.

A waterfront vista on the western edge of Calle del Sol where it turns the corner to meet Caleta de las Monjas atop the city wall.

Above and below: The same pastel façades that line Calle del Cristo grace Calle del Sol as well. Here the buildings are slightly more austere and mostly one storey. Below, the Baroque-styled balcony, roof line sconces, and moldings are the pinnacle of Old San Juan's most ornate colonial architecture.

CALLE DEL SOL

One block north of the Cathedral and perpendicular to Calle del Cristo, is still one of Old San Juan's romantic streets, this one known as **Calle del Sol**.
The **longest street in the historic district**, Calle del Sol bisects Old San Juan from east to west and, like Calle del Cristo, is lined with the single and multi-storied stucco buildings that the old city is identified with.

Above: An aerial view of the Plaza de San José located at the end of Calle del Cristo where it meets Calle San Sebastián. The plaza itself is centered around the large white mission-styled building in the background of the photo. The yellow stuccoed Ballajá Barracks are just visible in the top left corner.

Left: A close-up of a chapel cupola, inside the Iglesia de San José, just to the rear of the plaza.

Right, top and bottom: The main square of the plaza with its centerpiece: a statue dedicated to Puerto Rico's first governor, Juan Ponce de León.

PLAZA DE SAN JOSÉ

Where **Calle del Cristo** intersects with **Calle San Sebastián** on the northern slope of Old San Juan sits the **central square** of the historic district, the **Plaza de San José**. In the center of the Plaza is a **statue of Juan Ponce de León**. Cast in iron, the sculpture was reportedly made from melted down English cannons, guns which the invaders dispossessed after a failed attack on El Morro in the 16th Century. The buildings surrounding the Plaza include several of Old San Juan's most historic attractions. They include the **Iglesia de San José**, where the conquistador's coat of arms is honorably displayed; the **Museo de Pablo Casals**; and the **Casa de los Contrafuertes**, also known as the **House of the Buttresses**.

Left: The atrium of the Dominican Convent off Plaza de San José where concerts, plays, and festivals are frequently held and the soothing music of Gregorian chant fills the air.

Above: On display inside the historic Pharmacy Museum are hundreds of ceramic canteens used through the 19th Century to mix, distill, and store medicines for the residents of San Juan.

DOMINICAN CONVENT

The **Dominican Convent**, built in 1523, is also set off of the Plaza. Dominican friars lived here until 1838 when it was converted into army barracks. During periods of occupation the Convent also served as barracks for foreign troops, including the Americans, who used it for their headquarters until 1966. Today the Dominican Convent houses a library and belong to the **Institute of Puerto Rican Culture**. The indoor patio of the convent is often used for **outdoor concerts** and **plays**. The interior decor has been preserved wherever possible to resemble the Convent's 16th Century origins. One is likely to hear the music of **Gregorian chants** undulating through the halls and passageways.

CASA DE LOS CONTRAFUERTES

Also located on **Calle San Sebastián**, off the Plaza de San José is the **Casa de los Contrafuertes**, **House of the Buttresses**. Not surprisingly, the house takes its name from the thick buttresses which are its support system. Also dating back to the 16th Century, the house claims to be the oldest residence in Puerto Rico although Casa Blanca is officiated as such. Today the Casa de los Contrafuertes houses the **Pharmacy Museum**, shown above, which was a working apothecary through the 19th Century. Old San Juan's **Graphic Arts Museum** occupies the upper floor of the house and displays a wide variety of works by local artists.

MUSEO DE PABLO CASALS

One of Puerto Rico's most revered sons was the Spanish born cellist, composer and conductor, **Pablo Casals**. Born in 1876, Casals had earned international renown by the time he was 23, particularly for his interpretations of the German masters. He immigrated to Puerto Rico in 1957, where he lived until his death in 1973. The museum which bears his name houses a number of his **manuscripts**, an **original instrument** used by the maestro, as well as several **videos** and **recordings** of his greatest works. A charming 18th Century-styled house, the **Museo de Pablo Casals,** is located on Calle San Sebastián, just off the square of Plaza de San José. **The Casals Music Festival**, which he founded shortly after his arrival in Puerto Rico, takes place here every year in June. It was, and still is, considered to be one of the Caribbean's most important cultural events.

An interior view of the Iglesia de San José located off the Plaza de San José.

Below: The entrance to the museum dedicated to Puerto Rico's most famous musician: cellist, conductor, and composer Pablo Casals, is located off the main square of the Plaza de San José.

Various representations of Puerto Rico's indigenous arts and crafts on display throughout Old San Juan's many museums and gift shops.

ARTS AND CRAFTS

Old San Juan offers a virtual melange of artistic craft and **objet d'Art** for souvenir collecting tourists to revel in. Visit the **Museo de Santos**, **Museum of Saints**, which displays a wide collection of **saint carvings**. Usually done in wood, clay or stone, the carvings were often brightly painted with vegetable dies.

They were used by the conquistadors and missionaries as token offerings to the native Indians in order to persuade them to convert to Christianity. Other indigenous art crafts worth collecting include the Puerto Rican weaving known as *mundillo* or **lacemaking**, which today exists only in Spain and on this island. The *torchón*, or **beggars lace** version is

particularly popular. Puerto Rico is also famous for the craft of **mask making**. The so-called *caretas* are **paper maché** or **coconut husks masks** worn by the residents during festivals. Though these masks were traditionally worn in medieval Spain, Puerto Rico's versions bear the influence of the island's **African heritage** as well. For an even more comprehensive study of the arts and crafts of San Juan visit the **Institute of Puerto Rican Culture** inside the Dominican Convent. If this were not enough, visit any one of the numerous **antique shops** or **modern art galleries** along Calle del Cristo. Most of them display the works of contemporary Puerto Rican artists, like the painter **Angel Botello** who died in 1986.

CASTILLO DE SAN CRISTÓBAL

Dating a century after its older sister to the west, the military fortress known as the **Castillo de San Cristóbal** stands on the opposite end of Old San Juan from El Morro, guarding the **northeastern side** of the old city. Begun in 1624, this companion fortress was erected to aid against land-based attacks on El Morro's weaker flank, like that launched from Condado by the British in the 16th Century. It was completed over fifty years later, in 1678. Unlike El Morro, however, San Cristóbal was not designed by Spaniards, rather by a pair of **Irish expatriots** employed by the Spanish crown. Nicknamed the **"Wild Geese"**, **Alejandro O'Reilly** (a special emissary of the King who also consulted the crown on fiscal and administrative policies) and **Thomas O'Daly** employed some of the same engineering acumen that existed at El Morro: **multi-tiered**

ramparts, **interior sub-forts**, **steep artillery ramps**, and **tunnels**. The massively fortified **exterior walls** complete with the unique *garitas* ultimately connect San Cristóbal to El Morro, thus completing the security belt around the **"walled city"**.

Although it is, in size, smaller than El Morro, San Cristóbal stands a bit taller, rising just over 150 feet above sea level. El Morro is only 140 feet high. Small difference though it is, the Irishmen must have been keen to something, for, unlike the older fort, San Cristóbal was never, ever overrun.

As at El Morro there is a **museum** exhibit at San Cristóbal, as well as a video presentation which portrays the life of the soldiers that stood guard here in the 17th and 18th Centuries. Like El Morro, San Cristóbal eventually came under administration of the Americans and remains today under the operation of the U.S. National Park Service.

An aerial view of the northern peninsula of Old San Juan looking east towards the metropolitan area with the magnificent Castillo de San Cristóbal, sister fortress to El Morro, visible in the foreground.

A beautifully inscribed cannon, no doubt dedicated to her noble Spanish patron, faces east directly in line with San Juan's current capitol building whose brilliant white dome is visible in the distance.

Above: Yet another of San Cristóbal's mighty armaments, this one pointing due south, in the direction of the harbor.

Left: Colonial ammunition, stacked symmetrically along one of San Cristóbal's many ramparts.

CANNON EMPLACEMENTS

As at El Morro, the **exterior walls** of San Cristóbal are beveled by the **angled spaces** where **cannons** were once installed. Shown above, a cannon and its artillery remain on display within the fort walls. The cannon itself still rests in its original firing position, this one pointing down from San Cristóbal south, towards the city and its harbor.

As at El Morro, San Cristóbal has an impressive **central courtyard** known as **Plaza de Armas**. It means, quite appropriately, **"of arms"**. This plaza, if not larger than the one at El Morro, is at least more open. There is a **vaulted arcade** which surrounds the **grey and red checkered floor pattern** of the courtyard. With matching red brick tiles on the **upper ramparts**, these aesthetic touches give San Cristóbal a grander presence than the yellow and white relief vaulting along El Morro's courtyard walls. **San Cristóbal's museum** also displays **written** as well as **video histories** of the fort and is located off the central courtyard. Visitors can also see displays of the **uniforms** fashioned by the colonial soldiers, some one hundred years after their compatriots at El Morro.

CAPILLA DE SANTA BÁRBARA

Of course the soldiers at San Cristóbal had to have a place to worship, as well as a sanctuary in which to seek blessings of strength before a battle. Interestingly enough, their **chapel**, unlike the one at El Morro, is not hidden within the forts walls but located directly off the Plaza de Armas inside the main courtyard. Known as the **Capilla de Santa Bárbara**, the small sanctuary is painted in a **subtle yellow pastel** adding still another dimension to the architectural elements of San Cristóbal's interior. Simple and small, it has a plain altarpiece decorated with only a simple statue of Santa Bárbara.

GARITAS

The *garitas* or **sentry boxes** employed at El Morro are just one of the technical elements borrowed by the "Wild Geese" for use at San Cristóbal. As at El Morro or even La Fortaleza, the *garitas* dot the outer walls of San Cristóbal marking the station points where individual soldiers once stood guard.
There is one in particular, known as the **Garita del Diablo**, the **Devil's Sentry Box**, which sits at the end of San Cristóbal's longest tunnel, all the way out to the edge of the waterfront. It takes its name, one could imagine, from the especially **isolated position** of this outpost making it a more vulnerable position than other stations at the fort. What ever the case may be, the Garita del Diablo also offers some of the best ocean and **shoreline views** in all of Old San Juan.

On the following pages:
Top left: A view of San Cristóbal's central courtyard, Plaza de Armas, and its arcade from the upper ramparts. Both are decorated with a beautiful, albeit faded, grey and red tiling. Below left: Another view of the Plaza de Armas from inside the plaza arcade looking out towards the quaint yellow sanctuary known as the Chapel of Santa Bárbara, where soldiers of San Cristóbal once found their religious inspiration and reprieve.

Below: A view from one of San Cristóbal's upper ramparts, looking east over the metropolitan area. As at El Morro, San Cristóbal employs the individual garitas, or sentry boxes, where soldiers once stood watch over the Atlantic shore.

Top right: The austere interior of the Chapel of Santa Bárbara, looking out onto the fortress plaza. Below right: Colonial uniforms once worn by the Spanish soldiers stationed here on display inside San Cristóbal's museum.

Componentes del uniforme español de infantería – Siglo XVIII
Components of a Spanish infantry uniform – 18th. Century

PLAZA DE ARMAS

Located in the heart of Old San Juan at the corner of Calle Fortaleza and Calle San José, is another plaza titled **Plaza de Armas**. Modeled after a similar setting in Madrid, this plaza containing San Juan's **Alcaldía**, the historic seat of the local magistrate was completed in the mid-19th Century. Like most of the buildings surrounding Plaza de Armas, the Alcaldía looks distinctly **neo-classical**; many have **arcades** or are topped by Cathedral-like **towers**. The **Intendencía**, which houses the **U.S. State Department**, is also on the Plaza. As with many other open plazas in Old San Juan, Plaza de Armas was once used as a drill field for the Spanish soldiers stationed here.

Preceding pages: The spectacular vista seen from the Garita del Diablo, the Devil's Sentry Box, which sits at the very end of San Cristóbal's longest tunnel. It offers one of the most dramatic coastal views in all of San Juan.

Left: The Alcaldía, seat of the local magistrate, located off the Plaza de Armas in Old San Juan. The plaza was modeled after a similar square in Madrid.

Bottom: This is the Teatro Tapia y Rivera, located on the southern side of Plaza de Colón. Named after a famous Puerto Rican playwright, the theater houses various concerts, operas, and dance performances.

Above: The neo-classical design of San Juan's capitol building, known as El Capitolio, is resemblant of the U.S. Capitol building in Washington D.C. after which it was modeled.

PLAZA DE COLÓN

The **Plaza de Colón**, also known as **Columbus Square**, is located at the extreme eastern edge of Old San Juan serving as a sort of ad hoc **gateway** from Old San Juan to **the metropolitan area**. It is, as its name would indicate, dedicated to the explorer that first discovered this Antilles island in 1493, Christopher Columbus. A large **statue of Columbus** stands in the very center of the square, placed there in 1893 to commemorate the 400th Anniversary of his arrival.

TEATRO TAPIA Y RIVERA

On the south side of the Plaza de Colón is the **Teatro Tapia y Rivera**, also built in the mid-19th Century. Less ornate than other buildings in Old San Juan, the theater is a minimalist box, with the barest of neo-classical façade trimmings. It was named for the famous Puerto Rican **playwright**: **Alejandro Tapia y Rivera** who died in 1882. A wide variety of theater arts besides plays

are performanced at Teatro Tapia, including **musical concerts, operas, dance performances**, and other cultural events.

CAPITOL BUILDING

Though it is technically situated in **San Juan metropolitan area**, along the northern coast just east of the historic district, the city's modern day **capitol building**, **El Capitolio**, can be seen from most of Old San Juan's higher vantage points. For example, its enormous **white cupola** can be seen from San Cristóbal's upper ramparts. Built between 1925 and 1929 it bears striking resemblance to the U.S. Capitol in Washington D.C. As such, it stands as a prominent symbol of the modern importation of **American aestheticism** after Puerto Rico's status as a U.S. Commonwealth was officiated. Even still, Puerto Rican nationalism is equally represented here. The island's **coat of arms** is prominently displayed in the form of a **stained glass mosaic** inside the building and the official **Puerto Rican Constitution** sits behind glass to be read by observers.

Left: One of San Juan's ubiquitous cruise ships at port off Calle de la Marina in Bahía de San Juan with the capitol building visible in the background.

Above: A panoramic of the harbor shows San Juan's busiest piers, the ports-of-call for many cruise ships, off Calle de la Marina. They alone have secured San Juan's age-old reputation as "the first and last safe harbor of the Caribbean".

THE HARBOR

As in the colonial era, the **port of San Juan**, **Bahía de San Juan**, is the most heavily used port in all of the Antilles. It remains, as it was known then, as "the first and last safe harbor of the Caribbean". Today, of course, the vessels ferrying in and out of these inlet waters are **commercial freighters** rather than Spanish galleons and, even more often than that, they are **recreational cruise ships**. The piers that front the southern coast of Old San Juan on **Calle de la Marina** are the resting place for cruise ships like the **Royal Caribbean** cruise line, which transport adventure seeking tourists in and out of San Juan almost daily. Follow their lead and take a ferry from Pier Two across the harbor to the **Barrilito** or **Bacardi rum**

distilleries at **Cataño**, or charter a fishing vessel for a day of **tropical deep sea fishing**. If you are lucky, you could even go **SCUBA diving**. The **U.S. Customs House**, located at the end of the Calle de la Marina, is a prominent and surprisingly attractive pink and white **faux neo-colonial structure** meant to blend with the rest of Old San Juan. The city of San Juan is spending **several hundred million dollars in renovating** the rest of the piers. The works will be completed by 1997. Titled **Frente Portuario**, it will be a complete shipping and tourist complex, including residential condominiums, a hotel and casino, while retaining the neo-colonial architectural features of Old San Juan.

Left: A view of some of San Juan's glittering resorts in the region known as El Condado. Beautiful beaches, recreational parks and the spectacular Condado Lagoon, just visible to the right, make this one of the biggest tourist attractions in all of Puerto Rico.

Above: An aerial view of the lagoon itself, literally encircled by high rise hotels and luxury condominiums. The lagoon provides one of the most beautiful resort settings on the island.

EL CONDADO

Further east of Old San Juan but still along the northern coast is a vast collection of **glittering resorts** and **residential condominiums** known as **El Condado**. El Condado means literally **The County** and it represents all that is good and bad about San Juan. It is a development area resemblant of Hawaii's Waikiki or Florida's Miami beach. For the sake of its unique location, sandwiched between the Atlantic coast and the lovely **Condado Lagoon**, some observers have complemented it as beautiful still others think it is ostentatious and overly commercial. Whatever the opinion, there are some wonderful things to experience here, namely the **beaches** and a number of **recreational parks**.
Filled as it is with **shopping boutiques**, **four star**

restaurants, **bars** and **discos**, El Condado is a tourist magnet, with most of these places located on its main street, **Ashford Avenue**, while still others are located on resort premises. Some resorts, like the Condado Plaza, the Radisson and the Marriott resort host **casinos** as well. But if glitz is not what you seek, go elsewhere.
East of these establishments, on the other side of the bridge is the one resort hotel that is deliberately slower paced: the **Caribe Hilton**. With several acres of landscaped lawns and decidedly nicer beaches, the Hilton sits on the site of the historic **Fort San Gerónimo** and **museum**. A lesser military installation than El Morro or San Cristóbal, San Gerónimo was hardly less strategic in casting off foreign invaders. Adding a significant historical

element to the resort's atmosphere, the Hilton's setting makes for a much richer cultural experience. Still, as in Old San Juan, there are plenty of **waterfront promenades** on which to take a romantic stroll. If the glitz of El Condado is still too much, travel east of "the County" to **Ocean Park**, which furnishes a more spacious (simply meaning less crowded) beach and is generally slower paced.

Left: As in Old San Juan, El Condado is surrounded by a waterfront promenade that encircles the lagoon. In the evenings, under the lamplight, it lays further claim to San Juan's notorious romanticism.

Right: This monument, located along the lagoon promenade, is dedicated to Ramón Baldorioty de Castro, a delegate to the Spanish Parliament who founded the island's Autonomist Party in 1887. Although the island's independence from Spain was nullified by U.S. annexation, Baldorioty de Castro is still considered a hero here for his fight to abolish slavery and to establish the island's first constitutional bill of rights.

Bottom left and right: More condominiums and hotels along the lagoon in El Condado.

Above: An example of the beautiful palm tree-lined beaches that have made the district of Isla Verde a tourist hub second only to El Condado.

Preceding pages: Yet another example of Puerto Rico's most popular landscapes is also one of San Juan's last uncorrupted beaches. This one, in the district known as Piñones, is due east of the city and past Isla Verde.

Top right: As at El Condado, condominium development in Isla Verde has become the backdrop to many of its lovely oceanside beaches.

Below right: More luxury condominiums, favored by Isla Verde's population of retirees.

ISLA VERDE

Still further east of Ocean Park is the suburb of **Isla Verde**, so named for the actual island just off its Atlantic coast. On the interior side of the suburb is the **Laguna San José**, the **San José Lagoon**. The potential charm of Isla Verde has been corrupted by Puerto Rico's **international airport** located east of this area. Not surprisingly, hotels soon followed. The **beaches** of Isla Verde have as at El Condado, been overrun with tourists and this suburb is a favorite community for Puerto Rico's retirees. It is a relatively affluent neighborhood and Isla Verde boasts some of San Juan's **choicest restaurants** and **night spots**. Of particularly renown is the restaurant **Dar Tiffany**, which makes the uninspiring commute to Isla Verde worthwhile. Dar Tiffany was a favorite spot of the late actor **Raul Julia**, one of Puerto Rico's most revered native sons.

PIÑONES

Stretching down the coast from Ocean Park and Isla Verde is still another of San Juan's most popular beaches. Known as **Piñones**, the famous surf here is a by product of the **coral reefs** of **Boca de Cangrejos**. More than any other, Piñones is a **surfing** and **windsailing** haven for young people eager to test their skills riding the waves. Of course it is often very crowded, but certain stretches of beach, including the area known as **Playas Punta las Marías**, offer some of San Juan's most scenic spots. If you are lucky enough to get there on an off day, the long stretches of naturally white sand finished by a backdrop of overhanging palm trees, will remind you of a Caribbean postcard scene.

Left: One of the many stunning waterfalls located in the heart of El Yunque, Puerto Rico's own tropical rainforest.

Above: A view of El Yunque's dramatic tropical canopy.

EL YUNQUE

Travel thirty miles east of San Juan, and then turn inland from the northern coast just another five miles to the mountain region known as **Sierra de Luquillo**. Here visitors will find Puerto Rico's very own **tropical rain forest**. Referred to as **El Yunque**, the rain forest spans some 30,000 acres of the ascending mountain range, which peaks at over 2500 feet. Riddled with steep cliffs, El Yunque's topography is cut out by beautiful **waterfalls** and **lazy riverbeds**. Though diminutive by comparison, El Yunqe's skyward reaching **canopy of vegetation** is as dramatic as the Amazon.

Fueled by precipitation that sweeps in off the Atlantic, dumping close to 250 inches of moisture on El Yunque yearly, this **diverse ecosystem** has evolved into several **distinct forests** such as the **Colorado**, a coniferous forest, and the **Tabonuco** which is, surprisingly enough, a pine forest. This lush environment furnishes Puerto Rico with some of its most unique **indigenous fauna**, including the famed **tree frog** known as *coquí* and a species of deadly bacterial **river snails**.

For a tour of El Yunque start at the **Sierra Palm Interpretive Services Center** or the **Palma de**

Sierra Visitor's Center. Both furnish maps and information about the park. The **El Yunque Trail** will lead to many of the forest's best views including: **Los Picachos Lookout Tower, Mount Britton Lookout Tower, Pico El Yunque** and **El Yunque Rock**. Two waterfalls worth visiting are **La Coca** and **La Mina**, the latter of which can be seen from the **Big Tree Trail**. For the most complete experience embark on the **Tradewinds National Recreation Trail**. Stretching the length of the park, about eight miles, the trail is also known as **El Toro** and is the longest nature trail in all of Puerto Rico.

Shown left and right: Still more of the countless waterfalls that fill El Yunque, including La Coca and La Mina falls, which can be reached via the Big Tree Trail, the El Yunque Trail or even the El Toro trail.

Below: An example of the diverse vegetation that populates El Yunque which includes both coniferous and evergreen forests in addition to its tropical bush.

Above: To wander through a maze of wild palm trees as picturesque as this is just one reason to visit Luquillo. With wild coconut groves, genuine alabaster sands and crystal waters, it is no wonder Luquillo claims to have Puerto Rico's most beautiful string of beaches.

Top and bottom right: Aerial views of Luquillo expose its beautiful reef strewn waters. Above is pictured the same beachside palm grove from the photo on this page. Further down the coast and pictured below is a condominium complex resemblant of El Condado.

LUQUILLO

Directly north of El Yunque back on the coast is the lovely beach community known as **Luquillo**, named after the mountain range which over shadows it. Luquillo is, without contest, considered Puerto Rico's most beautiful beach. Its **alabaster sands** are lined with **healthy palms** and **coconut groves**, which no doubt thrive under the precipitation that drifts down the mountain side and irrigates this coast. Though the occasional mountain cloudcover can be a menace to sunbathers, it is also what has kept Luquillo so pristine. At either end of Luquillo are two similarly lovely beaches, **Playas San Miguel** and **Convento**. These two are considerably less

crowded than Luquillo, but put together they offer a sandcovered promenade over five miles long. With fewer resorts than El Condado, Luquillo still has a backdrop of **towering white condominiums**. If you plan to stay at Luquillo, try the inn known as **Parador Martorell**, located in the **ancestral home** of the Spanish **Martorell family**. Still owned and operated by the family's descendants, the inn is more of an upscale guest house or bed & breakfast than a four star resort. Relax in the flowering courtyard over tropical drinks, fresh island fruits, and home cooked meals. But best of all, the inn is just a five minute walk to this, Puerto Rico's premier beach.

Left: The beauty of Puerto Rico's beaches does not end at Luquillo. Further east and more remote is Cabezas. Here one can still find scenes like that pictured at left: a virtually cloudless sky, perfectly calm waters, soft pristine sands, and that perfect, solitary palm tree under which to rest one's head.

Above: A panoramic view of a beach at Cabezas shows its sands populated more by palm trees than people. Be sure to visit the Cabezas de San Juan Nature Preserve, which spans 316 acres of Cabezas' ocean waters and beach side forests.

CABEZAS

Further east of Luquillo, on the nubby peninsula just north of **Fajardo** is **Cabezas**. Like Luquillo, Cabezas offers some of the island's best beaches although the real reason to visit is the **Cabezas de San Juan Nature Preserve**. Surrounded by water on three sides, the preserve is probably the island's most eclectic natural habitat with 316 acres of **oceanfront lagoons, offshore cays** and **coral reefs, landbased mangrove** and **palm tree forests** and **flower beds**, not to mention an incredible collection of **animal life**.

A wide variety of **migratory birds** make their home here, as do an endangered species of **sea turtle**. Explore the **reefs** and **tide pools** for some of the most photographic sea life anywhere in Puerto Rico. First opened in 1991, this island treasure can only be toured with a guide and is meticulously cared for. Cabezas is sometimes referred to as **El Faro**, meaning the **lighthouse**.

The actual light tower, which stands out on a dramatic clifftop promontory, was built in 1880.

As with most of Puerto Rico's historic structures, the lighthouse is a charming **neo-classical building** and, like the one at El Morro, painted in shades of **black and white stucco. Panoramic views** from the lighthouse permit one to see for miles in any direction; westward and inland to El Yunque and the Luquillo mountains and to the islands of **Culebra** and **Vieques** to the east and south.

Above: Puerto Rico's largest and most luxurious resort, El Conquistador Resort & Country Club, is located on the island's eastern shore outside the fishing and yachting community of Playa Sardinera, near Fajardo.

Top right: Examples of the exquisite shorelines found on Vieques Island descriptively named Silver Beach, Orchid Beach and Half Moon Beach.

Right: The coast of Vieques Island, with the luminescent organisms which inhabit its waters and set the bay aglow at night.

FAJARDO

Beneath **Cabezas** is the next largest resort town and **sailing port** known as **Fajardo**. Sitting as it does on the nearest immediate landmass to the islands of **Culebra** and **Vieques,** as well as a good number of the **Virgin Islands**, Fajardo is one of the most popular ports-of-call for touring **sailboats** and **cruising yachts**. This has been Fajardo's status since the 18th Century, when it serviced pirate galleons and contraband-carrying trading vessels. Its commercial viability and strategical location made it a significant contention throughout the Spanish-American War of 1898.

Playa de Fajardo, which hosts the actual **marinas,** is at the east end of town. **Ferries** leave here daily for the islands across **Vieques Sound** including the more remote cays of **Icacos**, **Lobos**, and **Palominos.** Any of these make for a serene daytrip and potentially necessary break from the tourist traffic of the mainland.

The quaint fishing village of **Playa Sardinera** is just to the north of Fajardo which supplies an additional set of marinas, all of which are usually crowded. As at Fajardo, there are many good (though expensive) **seafood restaurants** here. This is also the location for Puerto Rico's largest and most luxurious resort: **El Conquistador Resort & Country Club.**

VIEQUES ISLAND

Vieques Island, directly southeast of Fajardo, is an isolated community of less than 10,000 people who still like to think of themselves as independent from the rest of Puerto Rico. With a much drier topography and more arid climate than the mainland, Vieques has earned several less-than-complimentary nicknames, among them: **crab island**, **useless island** and even just plain **small**. But none of these give credit to this tiny parcel of private paradise which, similar to **El Yunque** has a **mini rain forest** and herds of **wild Spanish horses** that have roamed freely over the Vieques hillsides since the 16th Century.

The island's two main towns are on opposite coasts. **Isabel Segunda** on the northern side, is the larger of the two, with most of Vieques' commercial outposts. **Esperanza**, a small fishing village is on the southern shore. Other industries in this largely agricultural island include sugar and pineapple plantations and cattle raising. The **beaches** here are especially nice, with romantic names such as **Green**, **Blue**, **Silver**, **Orchid**, **Half Moon** and **Navia**. Definitely visit **Mosquito Bay**, which is set aglow at night by **microscopic luminescent organisms** that live in the water. **Puerto Diablo**, on the island's northern shore is reputed to be the third point of the infamous **Bermuda Triangle**.

Above: This view of Culebra shows the island for what it really is a sprawling archipelago made up of more than 24 separate land masses punctuated by inland lagoons and whose large cavernous bays are peppered with offshore coral cays.

Above and below right: Two of the many bays on the island of Culebra which likely served as stopping point along the Caribbean trade route in the 17th Century. These same waters now cater to recreational yachts and commercial fishing vessels, as well as the U.S. Navy.

CULEBRA ISLAND

The smaller of the two offshore islands is **Culebra**, just a few miles north of Vieques and an hour by ferry from Fajardo. Not really an island as such, Culebra is actually a **mini archipelago** in itself, with 24 separate land masses in its proximity. The multitudinous **underwater reefs** and **coral cays** have made Culebra an oasis for **SCUBA diving** and **snorkeling**. Make the day trip just for this experience.

The crescent shaped port of Culebra, also known as **Pirates Cay**, was yet another important stopping point along the **Caribbean trading route**. Many of the island's beaches and inland areas are prevalent themselves in sea faring legend as reputed burial grounds for stolen treasures.

Claimed by the crown and donned as the **Spanish Virgin Islands** in 1886, Culebra was turned over to the Americans with the rest of Puerto Rico after the Spanish-American War, just twelve years later, in 1898. The town of **Dewey**, Culebra's capital, is actually named for a famous American naval commander, **Admiral George Dewey**. From the turn of the century on, much of Culebra was used as a **military installation base** by the **U.S. Navy** and after World War I as a gunnery range and bomb test site. This ended, however, in the 1970's after years of complaints from local residents fearful that the island's environment was being destroyed. Today the island is kept as the **Culebra Wildlife Refuge** and is operated by the U.S. Fish and Wildlife Service. As at **Cabezas**, several endangered species live protected here, including, **leatherback sea turtles** which lay their eggs on Culebra's beaches from May through July.

SOUTHERN PUERTO RICO

PONCE

Puerto Rico's **second largest city** is **Ponce**, on the southern coast. Separated from San Juan by the **Cordillera Central mountain range** which spans the island's width, Ponce was, until the last several decades, virtually cut off from the more heavily traveled northern side of the island. Its historic isolation has, over the years, cultivated a separatist and even, some say, elitist attitude among the **Ponceños** who insistently refer to their home town as **Le Perla del Sur**, the **pearl of the south**. While they can lay claim to the best weather in Puerto Rico–Ponce lies in the rain shadow of the Cordillera saving it from the precipitation that sets on the northerners–**Sanjuaneros** have wondered for years what else might breed such arrogance. But if there

is a secret to be kept in Ponce it won't be held hostage much longer. The massive interstate known as the **Autopista Luís Ferré** now connects Ponce to San Juan via a road cut through the Cordillera. Visitors can reach this secluded utopia in less than two hours.

Founded in 1692, Ponce was named after **Loíza Ponce de León**, great-grandson of Juan. Like San Juan, Ponce is famous for its architectural prowess. Though there is the same **neo-classical** and **Spanish colonial influence** that exists in Old San Juan, most of Ponce's buildings reflect a mixture of an indigenous style called **Ponce Créole** and the imported styles of the **Art Deco** period from the last century.

A daylight view of the elaborate Lion Fountain, located across the plaza from Ponce's Cathedral of Our Lady of Guadalupe which is visible in the background.

Above right and left: The pale blue and white stuccoed façade of the Cathedral, offset by its metallic cupolas, is as beautiful in the daytime as it is at twilight.

Below right: The interior of the Cathedral is as lovely as its exterior, exposing the mixture of Romanesque and neo-classical styles employed outside. The gold and silver inlaid altar and crystal chandeliers are unusual amenities set against the Gothic inspired vaulting of the nave and transept.

Following pages: The magnificence of the Lion Fountain lit up by night.

CATHEDRAL OF OUR LADY OF GUADALUPE

Directly in the center of town off **Plaza de las Delicias** is one of the most beautiful buildings in Ponce and the most important religious shrine in southern Puerto Rico. The **Cathedral of Our Lady of Guadalupe** was first built in 1660 and named after the **patron saint of Ponce**. It has been raised and rebuilt several times since then due to fires, earthquakes and other natural disasters. The current structure is a mixture of **Gothic** and **neo-classical styles** and was completed in 1931. Though the bulk of the building is painted in tasteful shades of **white and pale blue stucco**, the **towers** which flank the central nave off the **façade's** art are painted a **metallic silver**. Ostentatious though they may be, the towers efficiently reflect the sunlight which gleams off the waterpool of the famed **Lion Fountain** directly to the south of the Cathedral. Put together, it makes for a very dramatic setting.

Above: The unusual façade of Parque de Bombas, one of Ponce's greatest tourist attractions, is lit up (even in daytime) like a carnival fun house.

Above and below right: A pair of historic fire trucks, on display inside the building atrium, honor the legacy of the former Municipal Fire Brigade. Many of the men who served here are duly honored by the photographs which line the walls.

Below left: A close-up of the building façade betrays a virtual mosaic of eclectic ornamentation including fan-shaped windows, decorative shutters and eaves, and of course, stripes, stripes, stripes.

PARQUE DE BOMBAS

Also off **Plaza de las Delicias** at the end run of **Calle Cristina** is the architectural anomaly known as **Parque de Bombas**, the **Park of Fire-pumps**. This unusual structure, which looks, from the outside, as if it should be a wax museum or fun house, is actually the historic fire station of Ponce. Built in 1882, it was originally intended to be used as the headquarters of an agricultural fair, which might account for its unique design. Parque de Bombas is painted almost entirely in **red and black stripes** and bears garlands of **electric lights** from its roof that resemble Christmas decorations. The corners of the building have an **octagonal shape** and are peaked by **turret like roofs**. Even more eclectic is the **mini cupola** atop the building's central roof.

Shortly after the conclusion of the original fair, in 1883, the building was inhabited by the **Municipal Fire Brigade**. The year of its inception is lit up on the central facade. Proud as Ponceños are of this building's important history, were it not for the **antique fire trucks** on display in its open air garage, you would never know what this building was.

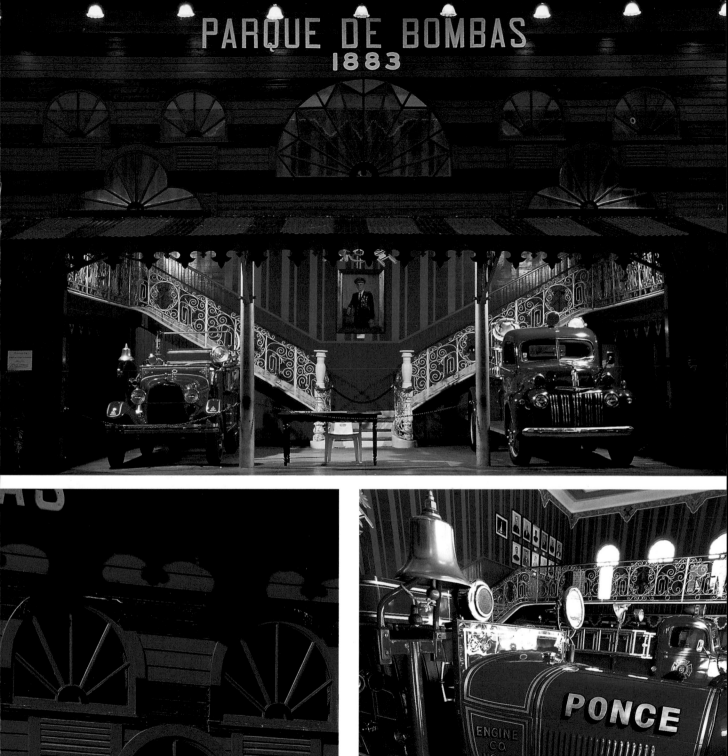

PARQUE DE BOMBAS
1883

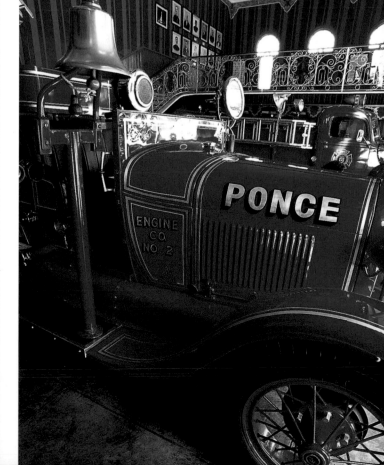

PONCE

ENGINE
CO.
NO. 2

The decidedly Greco-Roman style of Teatro La Perla, Ponce's center for performing arts, is distinguished by the massive Corinthian columns on its façade. This is the only part of building to have survived the massive earthquake of 1918.

TEATRO LA PERLA

Two blocks east of Parque de Bombas on **Calle Cristina** is the **Teatro La Perla, The Pearl Theater**, center of Ponce's performing arts. Originally built in 1862, the theater, like the Cathedral of Our Lady of Gaudalupe, was beset by earthquakes and fell to the ground in 1918. Distinct for its large scale **Greco-Roman design**, the only part of the theater that was left standing were the enormous **Corinthian columns** on its **façade**. The theater was not rebuilt until two decades later, but today, its condition is pristine thanks to a hefty **$450 million restoration project** called **"Ponce en Marcha"** completed by Puerto Rico's governor, **Rafael Hernández Colón**, a native of Ponce, in 1990.

MUSEO DE LA HISTORIA DE PONCE

Housed in the **former residence** of one of Ponce's favorite sons, **Dr. Guillermo Salazar Paláu**, the **Museo de la Historia de Ponce** is a unique and brilliantly designed exhibition of the **cultural, political**, and **industrial history** of Ponce. If Ponceños have a reason to brag about their Perla del Sur, it is surely on display here.
The original house was built in 1911 but the museum was not opened until 1992, to commemorate the city's 300th anniversary. It is located on **Calle de la Salud**, just around the corner from Parque de Bombas.

CASTILLO SERRALLÉS

Castillo Serrallés, a large **mansion** set two miles outside the city on **El Vigía Hill**, is the former home of **Don Juan Serrallés**, patron of the Serrallés clan, rum distillers extraordinaire and **one of Ponce's wealthiest families**. El Vigía Hill flourished as a suburb of the wealthy in the early 20th Century during the boom years of the **sugar industry**. The area is literally covered with mansions but Castillo Serrallés is considered to be the most exceptional. Completed in 1934, the house is often described as **Spanish Revival** in style and employs an unusual combination of **Moorish** and **Andulasian details** with **large courtyards**, **multi-terraced gardens**, **grecian pools**, and **panoramic views** of the city. The Serrallés family moved from the mansion in 1979 and in 1986 the city bought it to restore as a **museum**.

Right: The cozy entryway of the Museo de la Historia de Ponce. The museum is housed in the former residence of Dr. Guillermo Salazar Paláu whose day hats still hang on the wall.

Below right and left: Ostentation or class? The former estate of the Serallés clan, rum distillers extraordinaire and one of Ponce's first families, stands as testament to the wealth generated by the sugar boom in the early 20th Century. Its Moorish attributes, coupled with the grecian pools and fountains have made the house, which now houses a museum, an architectural spectacle.

Cabo Rojo Lighthouse stands a solitary watch, high above the treacherous cliffs of Puerto Rico's western shore.

CABO ROJO

Following the coastline west from Ponce and then further north after turning up the southwest corner of the island one comes to the coastal region known as **Cabo Rojo**. The region is famous for being one of the most remote beach areas of the mainland. Stretching for almost 20 miles, it is forged out of **rocky land based cliffs** and **reef strewn waters**. Severe promontories, like the one pictured above, required **lighthouses** to help sea faring vessels navigate about this region of the island's serpentine edge. But this is not to say that Cabo Rojo is without the smooth sandy beaches common elsewhere. On this, the Caribbean side of the island, there are also several flatter, calmer inlets, like **Salinas** or **El Combate Beach** which, despite the name, benefit from the absence of the Atlantic's fierce tides. Although vegetation is sparser here–the region, similar to Ponce, receives far less precipitation than other areas of Puerto Rico–Cabo Rojo also has a **Wildlife Refuge**. Just as refugees on the opposite side of the island do, Cabo Rojo's park serves as a protective habitat for many **island birds** and **sea life**.

The town bearing the same name is located some three miles inland on the western coast. Established in 1772, Cabo Rojo's town prospered from other island migrants that came here to work on the region's **sugarcane plantations**. **Fishing** is also an important industry, even for this non-coastal town. It is estimated that nearly half of the fish consumed on the island are caught off shore of Cabo Rojo. An annual **Fish Festival** is held here in February at **Puerto Real** which features arts, crafts and live performances that celebrate the fortitude of the sea and ocean life. There are fewer resorts on this side of the island but tourism is not entirely remote. Visitors will find nice accommodations at smaller hotels and other amenities including **golf courses** and **ocean recreation** such as **deep sea fishing charters**.

BOQUERÓN

South of Cabo Rojo is a large water inlet known as **Bahía de Boquerón**. Almost three miles in width, the beautiful bay is complemented by two additional lagoons: **Laguna Joyuda** and **Laguna Rincón**. This area is not as arid as Cabo Rojo and the immediate lands surrounding these lagoons are covered with **lovely mangrove forests**. There is still another wildlife refugee here, this one called the **Boquerón Forest Reserve**, which functions almost exclusively as a **bird sanctuary**.

The town of Boquerón is, not surprisingly, a bustling **fishing village** which has grown commercially in disproportion to its size in recent years. Fishermen here have been known to sell their catch to tourists right off the **Playa de Boquerón**. But other visitors come here purely for the sake of the waves; Boquerón has earned a reputation as the **surf capital of the west**.

Other interesting lore about Boquerón: villagers claim that the dread pirate **Roberto Cofresí** who once terrorized the island's seas, hid in a secret cave inside one of Boquerón's mini bays.

Right and below: Palm trees and mangrove forests grace the beaches and lagoons off the Bahía de Boquerón, legendary hiding place of Puerto Rico's most dread buccaneer, Roberto Cofresí. As for the trees themselves, they are home to one of Puerto Rico's premier bird sanctuaries inside the Boquerón Forest Reserve.

The beautiful central plaza of the village of San Germán looking towards the Renaissance-inspired colonial church of San Germán de Auxerre in the distance.

SAN GERMÁN

Visiting the colonial town of **San Germán** is, perhaps even more than Old San Juan, like stepping back in time. While other areas on this side of the island like **Ponce** and **Mayagüez** have grown and modernized, San Germán has scarcely developed. Its population stretches to reach 30,000. Set nearly ten miles inland from the southwestern coast, San Germán glows white against the unusually verdant hillsides which, over the years, have been used for the **cultivation of coffee**.

Originally founded in 1512, the settlement was destroyed by the French and then later rebuilt. In 1570 it was named after King Ferdinand's second wife, **Germaine de Foix**. During this colonial period it was the only other real city on the island other than San Juan and invading forces oftentimes made their outposts here, under the protection of the **Cordillera**, before advancing on the capital. Even more frequently, they retreated here after defeat. Of course it was not only military forces that armed

themselves here. San Germán also benefited from the piracy that ran in and out of Boquerón and the other westcoast ports.

More spacious than Old San Juan, San Germán has two large open plazas the first being **Plaza María Quiñones**, pictured above.

This venue might have formerly served as military training ground or commercial marketplace for the early settlers. María Quiñones sits just off the **church of San Germán de Auxerre**, so named for the French Saint which is the village patron. Unique to most **colonial chapels**, the steeple to San Germán de Auxerre is offset from the main nave and its **whitewashed exterior** is complimented by a striking **sky blue door**.

Like Old San Juan, San Germán is preserved by the lovely **pastel stuccoed buildings** which served as the colonial homes to coffee barons and settlers. As in the capital's historic district, San Germán has some of the best examples of traditional **Spanish**

One of the many plazas in San Germán where colonial residents conducted business during the day now enshrined with religious relics.

As in Old San Juan, the streets of San Germán are lined with the lovely pastel stuccoed façades emblematic of Spanish colonial architecture. These homes, however, employ less of the iron work amenities than their urban counterparts. More often these homes have large second storey wooden balconies, more quintessential of provincial residences.

architecture, in this case modeled most closely on the city of Seville.

But where Old San Juan's buildings are fixed close together and multi-storied, those in San Germán are more often **single storey buildings** set up along the hillsides in the fashion of the more **rural Spanish hacienda**.

Many of the homes are subdivided in the interior by delicately **carved wood screens** called *mediopunto*, an aesthetic attribute unique enough to draw architectural scholars from the outside world. On the subject of scholarship, San Germán is the location for one of Puerto Rico's international institutes of higher learning.

The **Inter-American University** is a small campus, it has less than 10,000 students but, considering that is nearly a third of the population of the town, it is not hard to understand why the academics have been so influential in preserving the cultural vibrancy and historic significance of this charming little place.

PORTA COELI

The Church of **Porta Coeli** is San Germán's second shrine and by far its most famous building. Built in 1606, Porta Coeli, meaning **Gate of Heaven**, claims to be the **oldest church in Puerto Rico**.

It is small and unrefined but that is exactly what makes it so lovely. In what could be described as **missionary style**, the interior support beams are exposed and, consistent with most of San Germán's other buildings, it is a single storey. The sides of the single chambered interior are lined with **statue bearing pedestals of the saints**, a significant element of Puerto Rican folk art. Still more are set inside portals along the walls.

The **altar** is uniquely recessed and separated from the half dozen or so pews by a banister.

It is decorated, like **Capilla del Cristo** in Old San Juan, by the paintings of **José Campeche**.

This alone is testament to the shrine's religious importance. Outside, the minimalist theme is completed by a frontal façade that is almost entirely bare. Its only decorations are the exquisite **medieval styled** *ausubo* **wood doors** which sit beneath a simplistic pediment.

There is no cross on the roof top, only a **cast iron bell**, leaving the church as a humble white stuccoed box floating atop a set of stone steps.

Top left: *The austere interior of Porta Coeli is simply accented by the statues which line the open nave and the José Campeche paintings behind the recessed altar. But the exposed beams along the ceiling and nave give Porta Coeli much of its missionary aesthetic appeal.*

Bottom left: *In the classic missionary style, Porta Coeli's façade is even simpler than its interior. The only ornaments here are its beautiful ausubo wood doors and the cast iron chapel bell which takes the place of a cross on Porta Coeli's roof.*

Above: *The Alcaldía, seat of the local magistrate or city hall, in Mayagüez. As with El Capitolio in San Juan, Mayagüez' Alcaldía was inspired by American architecture, in this case, the tradition of the Yankee colonial. The style is most apparent in the central clocked tower and cornice design. The sculpture directly in front of the Alcaldía is dedicated to Christopher Columbus.*

MAYAGÜEZ

The largest port on Puerto Rico's western coast, the city of **Mayagüez**, is also its **third largest city**. The city was established much later than most of the island's colonial settlements; it was not recognized by the crown until **Queen Isabella II** decided her ships needed protection for their passage through the treacherous waterways of **Mona Passage** off Mayagüez's shore. The town did not truly develop until the age of commercial and agriculture expansion in the early 19th Century. Today the commercial **tuna industry** is still its economic staple. Mayagüez is a young city and its image reflects this. There is no historic district to speak of. But although it might lack the architectural integrity of Ponce or of Old San Juan, Mayagüez makes up for it in **historic legend**. **Christopher Columbus** is said to have landed here shortly after his initial claim to Puerto Rico in 1493. A bronze statue of the explorer stands in the middle of the city's **central plaza**, **Plaza de Colón**. Mayagüez' **Alcaldía** or **city hall**, which sits off the square directly in front of the statue, is distinctive for its **American colonial design**. Mayagüez has an interesting church named for **Our Lady of El Carmen**.
Other landmarks include the **Mayagüez Zoo**, located one mile outside of town and **Mayagüez College**, which is a campus of the **University of Puerto Rico**.

Brightly colored fishing boats dot this shallow beach in Aguadilla, one of the few sandy spots along this predominantly rocky coast.

AGUADILLA BEACH

Rounding out the coastal communities of Puerto Rico is the northwestern outpost known as **Aguadilla**. Some twenty miles north of Mayagüez, this little resort community sits deep inside the basin **Bahía de Aguadilla** after which it was named. Aguadillans claim that it was here, in the protection of their corner inlet–the first repository off the gateway where the waters of the Caribbean and Atlantic meet–that **Columbus** first landed. A stream from which his sailors are said to have taken water is now the centerpiece of **Parque El Parterre**. The tourist industry is what sustains this community but, unlike other island towns, Aguadilla does not have the sense of being overrun. Its small scale resorts along the central avenue, **Avenida José de Jesús Esteves**, are surrounded by little parks. Any of the shops along this strip will probably be selling the *mundillo lace* that Aguadillan artisans have been making since the colonial era. This is the same lace one will see on display in Old San Juan. Visitors are not drawn to Aguadilla so much for the beaches since most of the region's coastline is rocky and jagged. In some places it is actually beachless. But **Playa Boquerón Sur** to the north is still a beautiful, albeit a shallow beach and usually littered with boats. Most beachgoers that come to this region are not even looking for a place in the sand, rather, a place in the surf. The town of **Rincón**, south of Aguadilla, is internationally renowned for its waves. In **1968** Rincón hosted the **International Surfing Championships** and has been known ever since as the **surfing capital of the Caribbean**.

CAMUY CAVES

Turning the final corner on the island, moving east just inside the northern shore one finds the town of **Camuy**, home to Puerto Rico's geological treasure, the **Río Camuy Cave Park**. The caves were formed deep inside the limestone earth along the bed of the **subterranean Río Camuy**, the third longest underground river in the world, over the course of several million years. Although the unique **chasms** are over **several hundred feet deep** in places and peppered with **stalactites** and **stalagmites**, the mineral rich soil and damp environment is known to furnish several varieties of **flora** and even full sized **trees**.

The most famous sinkhole, **Tres Pueblos** is over 650 feet wide and 400 feet deep, large enough they say to hold the entirety of San Juan's El Morro fortress. The **Taíno Indians** considered the caves to be **sacred ground**, evidenced by the ritual artifacts which have been collected from Camuy. **The Río Camuy Cave Park** is operated by the **Puerto Rican Land Administration** which opened the caves to the public in 1987. Over **260 acres** in size, it is one of the largest such preserves in the Western Hemisphere. The park grants access to four of Camuy's 16 known earthen repositories. After viewing a video explaining the caves' history and formation, visitors can experience this breathtaking system of millennial evolution via an **open air trolley** or along the foot path for a 45 minute **guided walking tour**.

Examples of the enormous subterranean caverns at Río Camuy Cave Park. Many of them are over several hundred feet deep, one is said to be large enough to fit all of El Morro inside it. Visitors, dwarfed by the caves' size, can experience these geological wonders on foot or by open air trolley.

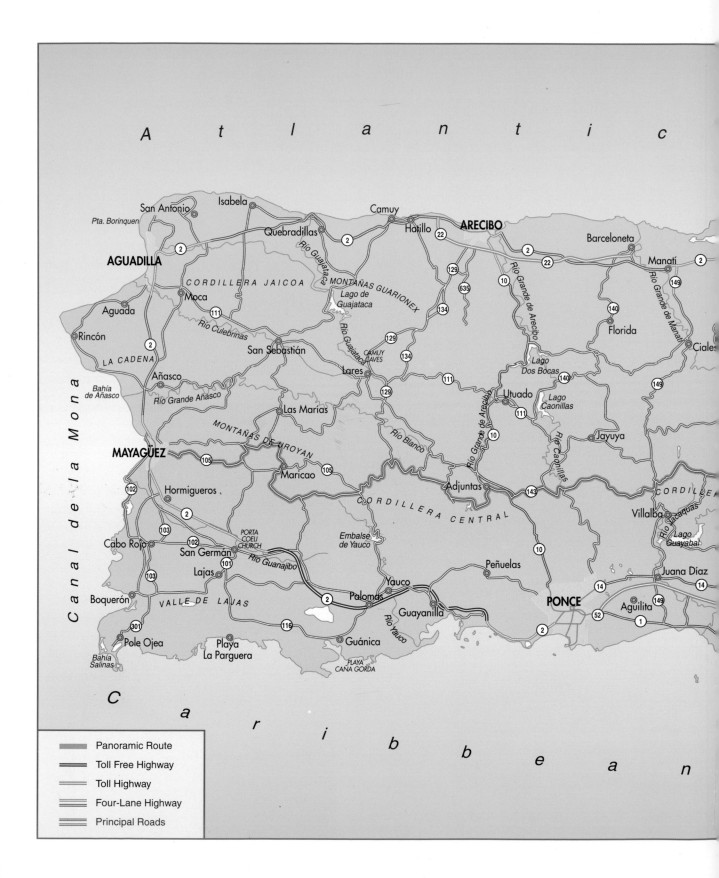

A t l a n t i c

San Antonio
Pta. Borinquen
Isabela
Camuy
ARECIBO
Quebradillas
Hatillo
(22)
Barceloneta
(2)
Manatí
(2)
AGUADILLA
(2)
(22)
(2)
(149)
CORDILLERA JAICOA
Río Guajataca
MONTAÑAS GUARIONEX
(129)
Río Grande de Arecibo
Río Grande de Manatí
Moca
Lago de Guajataca
(635)
(10)
(140)
Florida
Ciales
(111)
(134)
Aguada
Río Culebrinas
Rincón
Río Guajataca
(129)
CAMUY
CAVES
(134)
Lago Dos Bocas
San Sebastián
(149)
LA CADENA
Lares
(111)
Utuado
Lago Caonillas
Añasco
Bahía de Añasco
Río Grande Añasco
Las Marías
(129)
(140)
(111)
Río Caonillas
Jayuya
MONTAÑAS DE UROYAN
Río Blanco
(10)
MAYAGÜEZ
(105)
CORDILLE
(102)
Maricao
(105)
Adjuntas
(143)
Villalba
Río Jacaguas
Hormigueros
CORDILLERA CENTRAL
Lago Guayabal
(2)
Embalse de Yauco
(10)
(103)
PORTA
COELI
CHURCH
Peñuelas
Juana Díaz
Cabo Rojo
(102)
San Germán
Río Guanajibo
(14)
(14)
(101)
Lajas
Yauco
(149)
(103)
VALLE DE LAJAS
(2)
Palomas
PONCE
Aguilita
Boquerón
(52)
(1)
(301)
(116)
Guayanilla
(2)
Pole Ojea
Playa
La Parguera
Guánica
Río Yauco
Bahía Salinas
PLAYA
CAÑA GORDA

C a r i b b e a n

Canal de la Mona

▬▬▬	Panoramic Route
▬▬▬	Toll Free Highway
▬▬▬	Toll Highway
▬▬▬	Four-Lane Highway
▬▬▬	Principal Roads

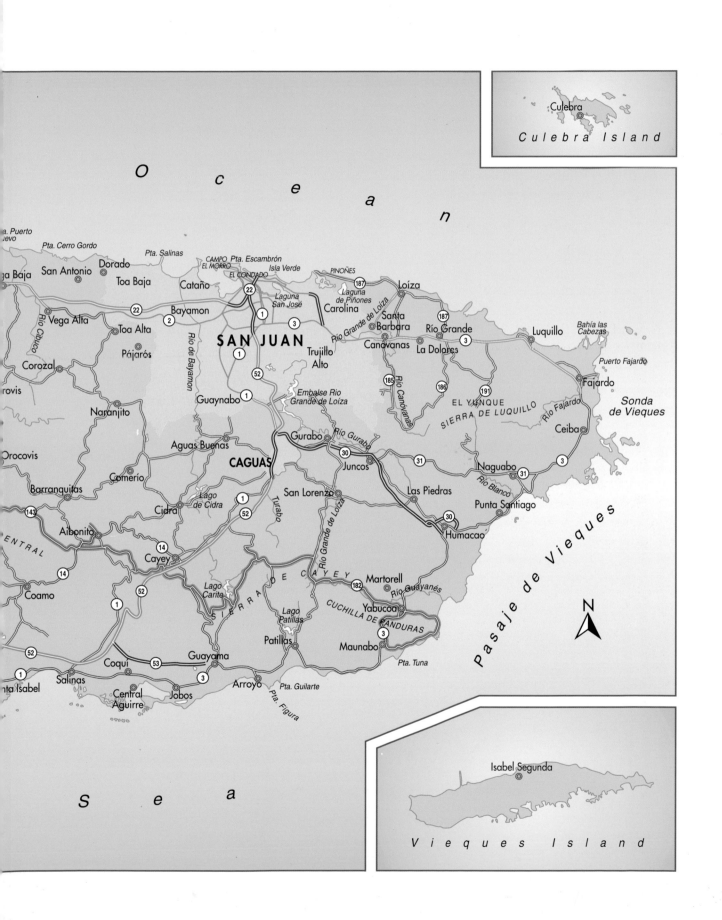

Culebra

Culebra Island

O c e a n

Ra. Puerto
uevo
Pta. Cerro Gordo
Pta. Salinas
CAMPO *Pta. Escambrón*
EL MORRO
Isla Verde
EL CONDADO
PINOÑES
a Baja
San Antonio
Dorado
Toa Baja
Cataño
22
187
Loíza
Laguna de Piñones
Bayamon
1
Laguna San José
Carolina
187
Bahía las Cabezas
Vega Alta
22
2
Río Cibuco
Toa Alta
SAN JUAN
3
Río Grande de Loíza
Santa Barbara
Río Grande
Luquillo
rovis
Pájarós
Río de Bayamon
1
Trujillo Alto
Canóvanas
La Dolores
3
Puerto Fajardo
Corozal
52
185
186
191
Fajardo
Naranjito
Guaynabo
1
Embalse Rio Grande de Loíza
Río Canóvanas
EL YUNQUE
Río Fajardo
Sonda de Vieques
Orocovis
Aguas Buenas
SIERRA DE LUQUILLO
Ceiba
Comerio
CAGUAS
Gurabo
Río Gurabo
30
31
Naguabo
3
Barranquitas
Lago de Cidra
1
Juncos
31
Río Blanco
143
Cidra
52
San Lorenzo
Las Piedras
Punta Santiago
NTRAL
Aibonito
Turabo
30
Humacao
14
Cayey
14
Río Grande de Loíza
SIERRA   DE   C A Y E Y
Martorell
182
Río Guayanés
Pasaje de Vieques
Coamo
52
Lago Carite
Yabucoa
CUCHILLA DE PANDURAS
1
Lago Patillas
Patillas
Maunabo
3
N
52
Coqui
53
Guayama
Arroyo
Pta. Tuna
1
Salinas
3
Pta. Guilarte
nta Isabel
Central Aguirre
Jobos
Pta. Figura

S e a

Isabel Segunda

V i e q u e s   I s l a n d

INDEX

PUERTO RICO
Project: Casa Editrice Bonechi
Publication Manager: Monica Bonechi
Picture research: Monica Bonechi
Graphic design: Serena de Leonardis
Make-up: Laura Settesoldi
Editing: Giovannella Masini *and* Patrizia Fabbri

Text: A. Carleen Hawn
Maps: Studio Mariani - Pistoia - Italy
Drawing on pages 8-9: Stefano Benini

The photographs belong to the Bonechi Archives and were taken by Andrea Pistolesi.

© by CASA EDITRICE BONECHI, Via Cairoli, 18/b Florence - Italy
Tel. 055/576841 - Fax 055/5000766
E-mail: bonechi@bonechi.it - Internet: www.bonechi.it

Printed in Italy by Centro Stampa Editoriale Bonechi.

ISBN 978-88-8029-493-1

* * *